ITERUM

OR A FURTHER DISCUSSION
OF THE ROMAN FATE

ITERUM

OR A FURTHER DISCUSSION
OF THE ROMAN FATE

BY

W E HEITLAND MA

CAMBRIDGE
AT THE UNIVERSITY PRESS
1925

Of London in 1778. '*Wisdom forms empires, but folly dissolves them; and a great capital, that dictates to the rest of the community, is always the last to perceive the decays of the whole, because it takes its own greatness for health.*'

Horace Walpole, 31 May 1778.

'*No Empire has ever persisted when the people at its centre forgot how to till the land.*'

Mr Lansbury quoted in *Observer*, 12 April 1925.

CAMBRIDGE
UNIVERSITY PRESS

University Printing House, Cambridge CB2 8BS, United Kingdom

Cambridge University Press is part of the University of Cambridge.

It furthers the University's mission by disseminating knowledge in the pursuit of education, learning and research at the highest international levels of excellence.

www.cambridge.org
Information on this title: www.cambridge.org/9781316633250

© Cambridge University Press 1925

First published 1925
First paperback edition 2016

A catalogue record for this publication is available from the British Library

ISBN 978-1-316-63325-0 Paperback

PREFACE

THIS little work is an attempt to raise a question of importance to students of Roman history in such a form as to provoke a plain answer. If the conclusions herein offered for acceptance are based on error, the sooner they are disproved the better. But I think that, if they are to be rejected, they should be disproved.

As I am not writing a history, I feel at liberty to avoid many topics of interest that do not seem necessary in presenting the main issue. It is not that I ignore them. Such for instance are the varieties of what I call the 'municipalities,' the exceptional Free cities, the relations of *municipes* and *incolae*, the cases of *attributi*, and so forth. And I am almost wholly concerned with the period of 27 BC to 284 AD, only glancing at earlier or later matters as occasion seemed to require.

It is perhaps rash for one who holds no official post licensed for the propagation of historical doctrine to come forward and ask a hearing for somewhat unorthodox views. I had better say at once that I have been accused of completely misunderstanding the Roman Empire by a writer signing himself or herself H M L in the *Journal of Roman Studies*. Only the wish to do my bit in the quest of true interpretation nerves me to face criticism once more. I do not like anonymous censure in general. But this condemnation may be the voice of some highly qualified lady or gentleman, member of a great University in which correct opinions find a ready market. So I appeal

to him or her for a clear and kindly refutation of my
errors, if he or she do not find it consistent with truth to
accept my views.

An article on the fate of Rome in the *Morning Post* of
26 Feb 1925 by Dean Inge impels me to add a few remarks.
He very naturally refers to the parallel case of Spain, and
speaks of 'the sudden decay of Spain after the reign of
Philip II.' The causes of this decay he finds almost as
obscure as the disease that overtook the 'Romans.' He
then proceeds to discuss various explanations that have
been offered for the decay of Rome; and his acute criticism
leads to the conclusion that separately or in combination
they are not adequate. A something remains unaccounted
for. So far as it goes, this conclusion seems to me just.
But I hold that it does not go far enough, and the reference to the case of Spain seems to me a good illustration
of the reason why. I believe all the pictures of Roman
strength and wellbeing in the first two centuries of the
Empire to be drawn from evidence that is inevitably one-
sided, and therefore misleading. I hold that the decay was
not sudden, that its beginnings must be sought much
further back than it has been the fashion to do, and that
there is evidence enough to justify my view. In order to
set this forth I have written the present work, as a sequel
to my *Roman Fate*. If I had referred to Spain, most certainly I should have cited it as a case in which the very
same error has blinded writers. The inner soundness of
the Spanish imperial system and the real wellbeing of the
Spanish people—after all, the kernel of Spanish strength,—
these are the points that need demonstration, before the
reign of Philip II. And I believe they are not demon-
strated, and cannot be.

The truth is, if I am not merely dreaming, that historic causes operate in steady and pitiless course. They sometimes escape the historian's eye because, working forward in the order of time, he meets with some phenomenon that appears sudden; in short, a contradiction of the scenes on which he has just now been dwelling. That his judgment should totter under the shock, is excusable. But every influence that weakens his grasp on the relations of effects and causes is a snare to him and misleading to his readers. He needs to look further back: how much further, nobody can tell. In so doing, he will probably find reason to reconsider his account of the state of things preceding the event that appeared so sudden, and end by being less convinced of its suddenness. This is what has been happening to me as a student, and I deem it my duty to confess it. Among the several hypotheses demolished by Dean Inge and others I have never met with a serious attempt to reconsider the prevalent view of the Roman municipal system and to treat it in connexion with the questions of land and labour, including slavery. Here is an inquiry that might be carried back to the very beginnings of civilization. On such a scale it is too large for a man of my age to attempt. But I think I can do something towards starting it on a sound footing. Even if I am convicted of error, I do not think my effort will be wasted.

TABLE OF CONTENTS

ITERUM

I

To record observed effects, and to trace the causes operative in producing them, is the main business of historians. And nothing more surely provokes further inquiry than the conviction that an admitted effect has hitherto been assigned to insufficient causes. I utter these platitudes by way of introduction to the consideration of some particular circumstances to which, as it appears to me, insufficient attention is generally given as an important contributory cause of the failure of the imperial system of Rome. That this system was in essence municipal, under a highly centralized control, is I think agreed. That in the period after the reforms of Diocletian we find it steadily going to ruin, in spite of legislative efforts that serve to record their own futility, is a commonplace of histories. Some writers wisely detect a prelude to this distressing scene in the events of the preceding century. To judge from our imperfect accounts of the hundred years following the death of Marcus in 180 AD, it seems amazing that the Empire should have survived the shocks, internal and external, to which it was subjected. Civil wars, foreign invasions, economic distress intensified by debased currency and by plague and famine,—surely these disasters are enough to account for the enfeeblement and decay that no Diocletian or Constantine could arrest.

Yet in blaming the calamitous third century for the incurable evils of the fourth we do not advance far in our search for causes. On further inquiry we are met by the remarkable fact that the first half of the third century was the classical age of Roman jurisprudence. So far as imperial machinery was concerned, the legal department was evidently in full vigour. Jurists helped in developing the Principate into an absolute Monarchy. Legislation by imperial rescripts or 'constitutions' gave prompt effect to the views of jurists. The murders of Papinian in 212 and Ulpian in 228 mark the military reaction against the great Civilians as Ministers. It would seem that under Emperors good bad or indifferent the nucleus of central authority remained in function, though probably at times hampered by the vagaries of individuals on the throne. Failure at the centre is not by itself an adequate explanation of the revolutionary movements of the age. Bankrupt finance and Provincial rebellions of military Pretenders are phenomena that invite us to look away from the centre; and this must lead us to turn our eye to the municipalities.

Now it can hardly be denied that the municipalities were severely damaged by the troubles of the third century, and that no measures of later Emperors availed to restore them to a healthy and prosperous condition. But, one asks, how came that period of troubles to arise? Was it a sudden result due to no apparent cause? Had the municipalities themselves[1] no part in producing it? It may seem so, if we are content to take the usual picture of their prosperity in the 'Antonine' period at its face value without question or reserve. This is just what I am not content to do. I am convinced that the municipal system deserves

---

[1] Even so admirable a work as Sir S Dill's *Roman Society in the last century of the Western Empire* does not seem (see pp 204—9) to face this question.

praise only in so far as its manifold varieties of detail[1]
serve to illustrate the wise reluctance of the imperial
government to impose a rigid uniformity of structure and
status on these local units. We must not forget that the
local governments had nothing whatever to do with
imperial affairs. They were not constituent parts, the
union of which built up an imperial whole, and gave to
that whole a character compounded of their several charac-
teristics. They were passive parts, subordinate to a central
power based on former conquest and present prestige;
their rights rested on grants from that power, and by its
leave they continued in function. With their local doings
Rome interfered seldom and unwillingly: any trace of such
interference suggests on the face of it that something was
felt to need amendment. If therefore we find the central
power intervening in municipal administration during the
second or even the first century, we have *prima facie* ground
for believing that all was not well with these local governments at a time when the *municipia* are supposed to have
been in their glory.

That there was such intervention is certain. The imperial
officers known as *curatores* were appointed by Trajan[2] to
check mismanagement of municipal affairs, a step surely
not taken without good reason by so careful an Emperor.
And it seems that they remained in function, gaining
power at the expense of the local authorities. It is there-

[1] See Reid, *Municipalities of the Roman Empire*, where this is fully
brought out.

[2] It has been thought that they were of earlier date. But the words
quoted from Nerva (Dig XLIII 24 § 3⁴) do not seem clearly decisive
on the point, unless we hold with Bremer that this jurist was defi-
nitely referring to the *curator*. In that case we get back to the time
of Tiberius.

fore no wonder that we find frequent reference to them
in the jurists of the Digest. Moreover it so happens that
in the correspondence of Pliny with Trajan we get some
notion of the sort of matters in which local authorities
were liable to go wrong and to stand in need of imperial
supervision. The chief points of mismanagement[1] were
as follows. The borough accounts were badly kept, and
the finances often in disorder. This was an old evil, dating
from the times before the municipal system had become
general, as we know from the letters[2] of Cicero. Public
works were undertaken without due consideration of the
suitability of a site or the use of proper materials, and the
evidence of local experts sometimes indicated that the
available technical advice had been ignored. Great sums
had in some cases been spent to no purpose. Meanwhile
services of obvious public utility, such as provision[3] for
the extinction of fires, were apt to be neglected, and
further damage resulted from such neglect. In one town
Pliny's Roman eye and nose detected an insanitary
nuisance, which he was eager to abate, if only the money
could be found for the job. This last condition was generally a difficult problem. The slackness of the municipalities, even in so plain a duty as the recovery of sums
owing to the *civitas* by its debtors, was scandalous. In
one case[4] a rent-charge on a town property had been
allowed to lapse, apparently for lack of repairs to the

---

[1] Plin *epist* x 17, 18, 23, 24, 37, 38, 39, 40, 41, 42, 43, 44, 47, 48,
61, 62, 70, 71, 75, 76, 84, 90, 91, 98, 99, 108, 109, 110, 111, with
Dr Hardy's notes.

[2] See Tyrrell and Purser's edition, Introduction to vol iii.

[3] Plin *epist* x 33, 34.

[4] Plin *epist* x 70.

building. Testators left bequests[1] to the towns, but it is remarkable that one man, a stranger to Pliny, chose to leave his money to Pliny upon trust[2] to employ the bulk of it at his discretion for the benefit of two *civitates* expressly named. In short, slovenliness and extravagance went hand in hand. There cannot be much doubt that these cities in Bithynia were nests of jobbery, and that the public chests were robbed by contractors corruptly appointed and protected by influential magnates. I need hardly cite instances of this form of corruption in Great Britain and the United States.

But it may be thought that the case of Bithynia was peculiar, and that things were better elsewhere. I know of no reason for such a belief. And in one of his private letters[3] Pliny shews that he had no such favourable opinion of some of the municipalities of his own neighbourhood in Northern Italy. A friend inquired how he could best secure the permanence of a benefaction made by him to a *municipium* (probably Comum). Pliny in reply points out that to make payment in cash will most likely end in the disappearance of the money: to do it by conveyance of real property (*agros*) means that the land, being town property, will not be carefully managed. He gives his own device for insuring the perpetuity of income from a trust. This plan he has found effective as a precaution against municipal mismanagement: but it necessitates a further sacrifice on the part of the donor. In such circumstances it is clear that the local patriotism of benefactors was exposed to severe strain. Yet this evidence comes

---

[1] Difficulties in the way of such *legata* had been removed by Nerva. Ulpian *reg* xxiv 28, cf Dig xix 1 § 13[6], L 8 § 6.

[2] Plin *epist* x 75. [3] Plin *epist* vii 18.

from a period in which the *municipia* were generally flourishing, when personal ambitions found vent in local politics, and popularity[1] was courted by benefactions of all sorts; a state of things of which numerous inscriptions still preserved supply an imposing record.

It is not irrelevant to note that the epigraphic record of benefactions, which constitutes the most important evidence of municipal wellbeing, belongs mainly to the first and second centuries, and refers almost exclusively to boons conferred on urban populations. That this was the line taken by most of such interested or disinterested beneficence seems also to be suggested by the prominence given by jurists[2] to the privilege of *inscriptio nominis*. Among the duties of a Provincial governor was that of seeing to the proper practice of this coveted distinction, in conformity with definite principles. The *opera publica* on which such inscriptions would appear were evidently for the most part buildings designed for the comfort and pleasure of the townsfolk, baths theatres amphitheatres colonnades and so forth; above all, aqueducts. The rivalry of neighbour cities, sometimes intense, stimulated extravagance outrunning the municipal resources. A *res publica*[3] fell into debt, and men of money could win no small local glory by coming to its aid. For contributions to the cost

[1] Tacitus *ann* IV 62 uses the actual expression *municipali ambitione*.

[2] See the title *de operibus publicis* Dig L 10 §§ 2, 7.

[3] O Seeck, *Untergang* II pp 162—3 has an excellent criticism of the benefaction system, pointing out that the temptation to rely on irregular windfalls was very demoralizing to local finance. On pp 169, 528, he insists on the prohibition of state-borrowings. Such were, he maintains, not allowed, the latest known being under Tiberius. State-debts arose from balances due to contractors and so forth.

of a work begun with public money entitled the donors to have their names inscribed on it, provided the amount of the gift was in each case stated on the record.

The urban character of Roman political institutions, clearly marked in the history of the Republic, was stamped on the municipalities. Therefore we can hardly wonder, if we find in them public and private munificence directed mainly or wholly to satisfying the requirements and desires of townsmen. But as we become more and more conscious of them as territorial units, actual owners of considerable landed estates, with jurisdiction over their several *territoria*, we are reminded that each of these units comprised also a rustic population. It comes home to us that here is a side of municipal administration of which we hear practically nothing from inscriptions, very little (until a later period) from literary sources, and only a few significant items from the jurists. Now to anyone who will but consult the indices of the Corpus this deficiency of epigraphic evidence bearing on agriculture will cause no surprise. Inscriptions relative to a vast number of professions and crafts survive in thousands, and are for the most part of urban origin. Those who seek records bearing on rural conditions will find but a sorry gleaning when they try to add anything of value to the selections of Dessau. A moment's thought will perhaps convince the inquirer that this is just what was to be expected from the nature of the case. The town is ever articulate: not so the countryside. Moreover, if urban elements dominated municipal life (as they surely did), what was there for them to put on record in connexion with their administration of the rural area of their territory? They would hardly record misdeeds or blunders of their own, and the rest

would be mere routine, of no particular interest. As to
literature, ancient writers are notoriously silent as to the
lives and feelings of the free labouring poor. In a slave-
holding world such indifference was natural. The poor
rustic invited attention if and when he rose in arms to
redress his grievances. But in the 'Antonine' period
things seem to have been generally quiet, until we hear
of a serious rising[1] in Gaul and Spain under Commodus.
And this event, whatever the circumstances may have
been, is not likely to have been due to trivial causes.

From the jurists we do get enough details to furnish
some sort of picture of the relations of municipalities to
their several land-areas. Thus we learn[2] that of estates
owned by *civitates* some were let to tenants in perpetuity
at a fixed rent (*vectigal*), a form of lease known later as
emphyteusis. These are *vectigales*, and the rent therefrom is
due so long as the lessees or their assigns enjoy security
of tenure. The object of this arrangement is evidently to
insure a safe and steady income for the state. Other
municipally-owned lands are put in the hands of cultivators on the same terms as are usually granted by private
landowners. These are not styled *vectigales*. That is to say
they are not leased in perpetuity, but for an agreed term,
and the instalments of an agreed rent (*pensiones*) are due
at agreed dates, according to the conditions of letting.
They are governed by the ordinary rules of law and local
custom. For instance, the tacit assumption of renewal

---

[1] The *bellum desertorum* of Lamprid *Commod* 16 § 2, Spart *Pescenn*
3 §§ 3, 4, Herodian 1 10.

[2] Dig VI 3 § 1 (Paulus). See also III 5 § 7[1] (Ulpian), XVIII 5 § 9
(Scaevola), XIX 2 § 53 (Papinian), L 16 § 219 (Papinian). Gaius III
145.

(*reconductio*)[1] by bare agreement (*nudo consensu*) is operative, as in dealings between individuals. The amount of landed estate owned by the *civitas*, and turned to account by it in these ways, no doubt varied greatly in different cases. But that it was an important part of local finance seems to be beyond doubt. Nor do we I think wrong the local magnates by suggesting that they sometimes used their powers for their own personal profit. Trajan at least refers[2] to their playing into one another's hands as a matter of course. In the case of land we must remember that a long lease tends to be 'beneficial': that is, in favour of the lessee. He has the upper hand in the bargain, since the lessor is primarily concerned to secure a stable income rather than large returns combined with risks. In perpetual leases these considerations are too obvious to escape notice. That members of corporations are tempted to grant beneficial leases to each other, English experience attests: and the appropriation of capitular emoluments used to be carried out thus. If then I am judging the municipal senates fairly, I proceed to inquire what would be the practical effects of such a policy of mutual complaisance in the earlier centuries of the Roman empire.

The cultivation of land went on in three varieties of system. A small owner might work his own farm with his own hands. A tenant farmer might manage a farm or farms of which he was lessee. A landowner might farm his own land through the agency of a steward (*vilicus*, generally a slave) in command of a staff of slave labourers. The first case seems to have been rare and unimportant in the second century; and it is not likely that municipal

---

[1] Dig xix 2 § 13[11] (Ulpian).
[2] Pliny *epist* x 38 *dum inter se gratificantur*.

senators were content to live so toilsome and penurious a life. The third plan was common enough, but it had two drawbacks. It could only be profitable on condition of watchful and intelligent supervision by the master, which was too burdensome to suit many landlords; and slaves were less plentiful in a time of peace. So the general drift of things was in the direction of letting to tenants, though this system too involved no small difficulties. The employment of servile labour in a greater or less degree was of course possible in any of the three cases. In this classification I am including the estates of individuals as well as those owned by a municipality. Landlords resident in the town were an important and influential class[1] from the days of the later Republic. Speculation in Provincial land was only one of their lines of enterprise, combined with banking and usury. As we now speak of the 'British Colony' in a foreign city, these *conventus civium Romanorum* recognized certain common interests, and tended to pursue them by mutual support. Out of such informal unions developed the oligarchic senates which were a standing feature of municipal constitutions under the Empire. At first mainly composed of Italians, this Provincial nobility became in course of time more and more local in blood and traditions, owing to the effect of extension of the Roman franchise, intermarriages, and manumissions. But there is no reason to doubt that in general they retained the hard-fisted grasping ways of Roman thrift. Some, transplanted to Rome as imperial senators, are said[2] to

[1] A point well emphasized by Kuhn, *Städtische Verfassung* p 68.
[2] Tacitus *ann* III 55. We must bear in mind that by this movement the local senates probably lost some of their best men. O Seeck II p 167 seems also to have this consideration in mind.

have had a sort of sobering influence on the debauched society of Rome. It was men of this type that dominated municipal life in the period from Vespasian to Marcus.

I picture to myself a conclave of such magnates controlling the affairs of a municipality and at the same time interested in getting the largest possible income out of their own estates. This I believe to have been the normal position of the *curiales*. In granting leases of the state lands it is not likely that they would forget their own individual interests. They could not only oblige each other by granting leases to members of their own body on favourable terms, but might improve the value of their private estates. For it would often be the case that one holding could be worked to more profit or with less trouble if another adjoining it were brought under the same management. Thus there was much to tempt members of the local *curia* to gratify each other in such matters, of course 'squaring' any who did not deal in land-speculations. In contracts for public works, farming out of tolls, lax collection of debts, and so forth, there were means of stifling opposition. And, beneficial leases once secured by such collusion, it was comparatively easy to keep what had been gained. Indeed such a system tended to perpetuate itself automatically. For, the larger a man's income, the better he would be able to court popularity by outlay on buildings entertainments largesses etc, and rise to the highest local offices in the gift of the burghers. The cynical combination of greed ambition and corruption that had once flourished in Rome and had brought the Republic to ruin, was the malignant growth of a political and social system unable to find an effective solution of urgent problems. Rome herself had found

some temporary relief in the New Monarchy through the
bloody surgery of civil wars. But the canker was not
cured, and nothing could be further from the intention
of an Emperor than to suffer the elevation of little local
monarchs in subordinate units of the Empire. So the old
republican model, dissembled into unreality at the centre,
was retained in the municipal constitutions. Local government gave a semblance of freedom and kept local ambitions
in employ. If municipalities were jealous[1] of one another,
so much the better for the central power. But the little
dependent republics thus created had not even the possible
tonic of imperial responsibility[2] to keep their politics
healthy. To me they seem to have followed the fatal pre-
cedents of Rome herself on a petty scale, and to have
begun this miserable process very early in the history of
the Empire. This phenomenon, scattered and varying in
detail, would not attract imperial attention until it became
serious enough to call for remedies. Hence I think it comes
that direct evidence of malpractices in connexion with
estates of municipalities is rare.

There is however some such evidence directly cor-
roborating the suspicion aroused by the appointment of
imperial *curatores*, to which I have referred above. In a
title of the Digest[3] specially dealing with the management
of municipal properties we find the following opinion of
a jurist. Whatsoever a man cannot lawfully do himself

---

[1] Illustrated in Dion Chrysostom *orat* 34, 38, 39, 40, 41. For
later period, by Libanius and Symmachus.

[2] In *orat* 34 (p 59 R) Dion rebukes the Tarsians for their foolish
jealousies, adding τὸ γὰρ προεστάναι τε καὶ κρατεῖν ἄλλων ἐστίν.
Mommsen cites also *orat* 31 (p 650 R) addressed to the Rhodians,
and Plutarch *praec ger reip* 10 § 9, 16 § 4, 32 §§ 8—12.

[3] Dig L 8 § 2[1] (Ulpian).

(*suo nomine*) he has no right to do through an agent (*per subiectam personam*). Accordingly, if a local senator (*decurio*) by substituting the names of others (*subiectis aliorum nominibus*) should be the actual farmer (*colat*) of public estates in breach of the law forbidding[1] decurions to be lessees thereof, the unlawful enjoyment should be cancelled (*usurpata revocentur*). That this *revocatio* is to be the duty of the *curator rei publicae* is clear from reference to that officer just below, and from another passage[2] dealing with the perpetual leases, which the *curator* is not empowered to cancel without the Emperor's sanction. Now here we have proof that mutual gratifications in the form of beneficial leases had been forbidden by law. Therefore the abuse had become so rife as to provoke legislation. Attempts at evasion, by employment of 'men of straw' as nominal lessees, were the sequel: the jurist steps in to counteract this device. Ulpian, from whom this opinion is cited, was murdered in 228. A reasonable allowance of time must surely throw back the earlier stages of this drama well into the second century as a phenomenon of the golden age of the municipalities. That Trajan's encroachment on the freedom of local governments was not lightly made, is shewn by his replies to Pliny. That fussy special-commissioner plagued the Emperor with trivial questions. Trajan, overwhelmed with the details of a vast empire, sometimes curtly declines to be bothered with such matters, and tells Pliny to settle them on the spot. A significant episode is Pliny's perplexity[3] in a certain

---

[1] *quae decurionibus conducere non licet secundum legem.* For the later laws cf Cod Theod x 3 § 2 (372 AD), XII 1 § 97 (383 AD).

[2] Dig xxxix 4 § 11[1] (Paulus), cf L 8 § 11 (Papirius Justus).

[3] Pliny *epist* x 54, 55.

financial dilemma. He is getting in the moneys owing to the Bithynian cities, but fears that they may lie idle owing to the present lack of opportunities for investment. After discussing possible measures to meet the difficulty—which may not succeed—he goes so far as to suggest a plan of sharing out the amount among the *decuriones* as a forced loan, obliging them to find good security for its repayment to the *res publica*. In view of the later policy of the imperial government towards the municipalities, this is a momentous proposal. But things had not yet driven Emperors to such a counsel of despair, and Trajan brushed the suggestion aside.

The situation as shewn in this case is so remarkable that it demands a few more words. Pliny had to recover moneys owing to the cities, evidently because the local authorities had neglected to do so. What honest excuse could there be for this neglect? He feared that the cash, when got in, would lie idle; because there was little or no opening for investing it in land. Why so? Were the present landholders so satisfied with things as they were, that they would not sell? If so, does not this indicate that they had feathered their own nests snugly? I wonder. Nor, he adds, are men ready to borrow from the public chest, at least at the current rate of interest; for they can get advances on these terms from private lenders. Therefore he proposes to try the effect of reducing the rate of interest on sums lent by the state, hoping thus to attract substantial men as borrowers. If this plan also fails, he hints at compulsion, a measure which would be somewhat sweetened by the lower rate of interest. Trajan only sanctioned the reduction of the rate, remarking that compulsory borrowers might not be able to find any investment for the money forced upon them.

It seems to me that there were grave difficulties in the way of finding openings for the reproductive use of capital in a large part of the Roman empire. No doubt the great ports were busy with the activities of maritime commerce, and some cities favoured by their situation carried on a flourishing industry. But it is easy to get an exaggerated view of the volume of trade and commerce in the old world, in which so much of the traffic was carried on in ships of small burden during only a part of the year, or in caravans on the backs of camels. The cost of road-transport was often more than trade-profits could bear. Only the navigable rivers were cheap avenues to markets. That material objects of vast weight were sometimes brought overland (as from the quarries of Asia Minor) is an achievement probably connected with the lavish use of slave labour. An estimate of the population[1] of the Roman empire at a given date, however scientifically reached, is hardly solid ground for further conclusions: but without something of the kind a quantitative estimate of commerce is apt to remain pictorial.

I believe that in the great majority of the municipal centres the operations and outlook of trade and commerce were mainly local. That is, though goods from afar found a way to them by the gradual movements of exchange, such towns were not primarily concerned with production of articles for distant markets. This I believe to be especially true of the western and northern Provinces. The East was richer in skilled trades. The African Provinces were famed chiefly as producers of foodstuffs. Egypt was and

[1] Beloch in 1886 estimated it at from 50 to 60 millions at the death of Augustus. From the figures given in Whitaker's Almanack for 1924 I gather that the same area now contains more like 200 millions. Of course the conditions are very different.

remained unique. I have met with nothing to shake my conviction[1] that the basic industry of the empire was the exploitation of the soil by the labour of a subject population, whether slave or free. The Romans of the Republic had for some two centuries directly or indirectly battened on the fruits of this vicarious toil, while farming industry in the most fertile regions of Italy was decaying. Roman emigrants carried the system into the Provinces, and with it Roman notions of property. Roman power protected and sanctified a hard social and economic creed, only suitable for stalwart free citizens able to stand up for their rights. Propagated in a world of subjects, it was a chronic moral disease. Self-governing municipalities on the Roman model were ideal centres for its development. To live on the labour of others, and at the same time to despise and maltreat the labourers, was the note of a civilization doomed to perish from within, the wages of sinning against human nature.

If corrupt leasing of municipal estates was a confessed abuse that had to be checked by law, and the slack collection of debts called for imperial interference, still these were not the only ways in which the policy of local magnates could favour the urban population at the expense of the territorial rustics. The Roman legions were recruited from the Roman citizens, chiefly those in the Provinces; Italy was practically ceasing to contribute to the rank and file. And it soon became usual to make men Roman citizens on enlistment if they were not so before. In course of time the superior fitness of rustics for military service led to the enlistment of fewer men from the towns, and the burden fell more and more on countryfolk. The

[1] Dill p 205 comes to the same conclusion.

urban populations, accustomed to an easy life among the comforts[1] and amenities of their towns and to an industrial atmosphere in which slave labour counted for much, tended to become idle shirkers, as the mob of Rome had done before them. Now, though the legionary ranks were mainly[2] filled by voluntary recruits, conscription was sometimes necessary. Moreover the volunteers were not always eager for the hardships of army life: it was the prospect of bettering their position socially and legally that attracted many, and the sturdy alien desired to become a citizen. Clearly there were two ways in which a free peasant could be drawn into becoming a soldier of the line. Either the present conditions of his life must be such as to make that of a soldier seem preferable, or he must be taken as a conscript. In both these alternatives there was room for the local government to play a part. That the sons of the poor *coloni*, small tenants or sub-tenants[3] of the state or of private landlords, furnished most of the local contingent, is highly probable. And these would surely be the pick of available workers on the land. That the levy of recruits could be so managed that one farm or estate should suffer more or less loss of needful labour than another, is obvious. That the local authorities did not find means of serving their own interests in such matters, is most improbable. In the case of the aliens

[1] That the softening influence of urban life was a deliberate appliance of Roman imperialism is shewn by such passages as Tacitus *Agr* 21, *hist* IV 64.

[2] Dig XLIX 16 § 4[10] (Arrius Menander, first half of third century).

[3] Under the later Empire, the necessity of retaining rustic labour caused this to be restricted. Instead of men, money was taken and used for buying barbarian recruits.

enlisted for the auxiliary[1] forces, the opportunities of shewing favour may have been even greater, as there was less to attract volunteers.

II

Holding these views, I am gratified though not surprised to learn that Professor Rostovzeff has put forth[2], and means to substantiate in detail, an explanation of the revolutionary disturbances of the third century, in which the Roman Empire came near to perishing. He finds the central fact of that dark period in the complete and open subjection of the civilian machinery of the Principate to the rough dominance of the military. The main cause of this upheaval he traces to the antagonism between the soldiery and the municipalities. The governments of the latter had long misused their powers to the disadvantage of the peasantry, from whom the army was still chiefly raised; and the smouldering wrath of the peasantry at length made the soldiery bitterly hostile to the towns. Hence a period in which the naked sword is supreme, Emperors suddenly rise and fall, Pretenders are many, great jurists in high office are murdered, and the municipal cities are great sufferers from the tyranny and license of the time. Only the strong hand of a Severus or an Aurelian could control or reunite an empire so shaken, and even Aurelian was assassinated. Civil government as restored by Diocletian was a recognition that nothing short of Oriental monarchy was henceforth possible. The old con-

[1] Who only received the Roman franchise on discharge from service.

[2] In *Musée Belge* XXVII (1923).

stitution with its local liberties had found its end in blood-
shed and anarchy.

Whatever may be the detailed proofs of Rostovzeff's
explanation, they must surely include a demonstration of
the causes that embittered the relations[1] between townsfolk and rustics, and produced the fatal results which
historians find it hard to understand. This demonstration
I await with eager interest. I have independently got so
far as to believe that the 'golden age' view of the municipalities rests mainly on evidence necessarily one-sided in
character, and to suspect that the municipal system con-
tained from the first germs of a deadly disease. For two
hundred years or more the mere might of an Empire that
stood without a serious rival was enough to protect its
passive units and to dissemble evils that menaced the
fabric from within. I attribute the decline of imperial
strength[2] partly to the inevitable development of disease
in the local units. They could not maintain or restore the
vigour of the whole, and in the later Empire we find the
central power squeezing the life out of the helpless parts.
The process thus viewed is analogous to the fallacy of a
circular argument. In the history of Rome it is a very old
story. The Republic, having drifted into a position in
which nothing but a thorough reform could have saved
it, went to ruin for lack of any practical means of peaceful
reform.

[1] Among the burdens of occupiers of land, the commandeering
of supplies on account of the passage of troops was vexatious and
liable to abuse. See Dig vii 1 § 27³ (Ulpian) and Roby's notes.

[2] O Seeck, *Untergang* ii p 161 speaks of a continual decline of
population in these communities about the end of the first century.
I can find no evidence of this, but I cannot disprove it.

III

In view of the financial distress of the later Empire and the constant preoccupation of the central power with endeavours to increase, or at least to maintain, the output of agriculture, it is necessary to speak of a question raised by Heisterbergk. He asks[1] whether the exemption from the direct land-tax, enjoyed by Italy under the early Empire, was not a cause of the unproductiveness of Italian agriculture. He thinks that it was, reasoning thus. That the formation of *latifundia* proceeded under the later Republic by the elbowing-out of former small peasant holders by the pressure of the new big landlords, we learn from tradition. The lands so acquired were wanted for parks pastures or game-preserves, so that the area under tillage was reduced. After the repeal of the Gracchan legislation, much land that had formerly belonged to the Roman state passed into the hands of the wealthy land-grabbers, and became their private property, liable to no tax. There was now nothing to hinder them from doing what they would with their own. Social and political importance was desired by such men, and to extract a maximum economic profit from their estates would demand more attention than they were ready to bestow. From this point of view the conversion of small owners into small tenants would not have suited their purpose. They did not want a lot of free peasantry on the land: such persons were out of place in the new-style countryside. This of course implies full acceptance of the traditional story—the big man was not content with the small man's bit of land: he also wanted his room.

[1] *Die Entstehung des Colonats*, Leipzig 1876, pp 63—78.

Therefore, when the elder Pliny declares[1] that *latifundia* have been the ruin of Italy, we must not construe this as referring to the effect of large-scale **occupation** (*possessio*), but to that of large-scale **ownership** free from land-tax. For what encouraged this non-economic development of wilful land-pride was the *ius Italicum*[2], the right of property in land subject to no public burden. This Pliny found already operative in Italy to the ruin of its agriculture. In the Provinces he detected the same process beginning to operate. He cites for instance the case of Africa. But Heisterbergk remarks that his words only attest the extension of *latifundia* there, not the evil effect of the process. Nero's confiscation of the six great African estates was surely not an attempt to improve agricultural conditions in the Province, but dictated by financial straits or imperial jealousy of great land-potentates whose possible disloyalty might become dangerous.

That there was, at least in the period from Nero to Hadrian, a marked difference in rural conditions between Italy and the Provinces, seems true. The evidence of Frontinus[3] is conclusive on one point. The boundaries of private *latifundia* and the *territoria* of municipalities (*res publicae*) often ran together. In the Provinces this was often a cause of disputes; in Italy seldom. Why this difference? Because, replies Heisterbergk, in Italy the latifundial system was practically complete, in the Provinces not so. Hence Juvenal[4] advises professional

---

[1] Pliny *N H* xviii 35, where with *iam vero* we are to supply *perdunt*, not *perdidere*.

[2] Mommsen, *Staatsrecht* iii 807—810, Marquardt, *Staatsverwaltung* i 91—2.

[3] In Lachmann's *Feldmesser* p 53.   [4] Iuv vii 106 foll.

pleaders who cannot make a living in Rome to seek a
practice in Gaul or Africa. This argument I take to imply
that the great landowners were not prone to quarrel with
neighbours of their own class, but were troublesome to
res publicae whose territories bordered on their *latifundia*;
which on the face of it is likely enough. It would seem
then that the orations on themes (*declamationes*)[1], which
employed Roman lecture rooms in the first century, in
which the ousting of the peasantry by the selfish rich was
a favourite topic, were unreal displays of ingenuity, at
least as referring to Italy. Heisterbergk argues that this
unreality is a proof of the disappearance of such cases
from the actual practice of Italian law courts. Perhaps:
but the great teachers of rhetoric were often men of Provincial origin, and need not have limited their pupils'
attention to Italian conditions. It is doubtless true that
Italy (at least in the most desirable parts) was more early
and more fully absorbed by *latifundia* than other countries,
and that *densitas possessorum* facilitated encroachments even
on sacred precincts still belonging to the Roman People.
So says Frontinus[2], and the occasional revelations some
three centuries later in the letters and reports of Symmachus shew the permanence of this state of things.

Now while Italy (with exception of certain hill-districts)
had become a country of land held in large blocks, property of municipalities or rich individuals, how did things
stand in the Provinces so as to account for the difference
noted above? It was a general rule that Provincial land,
strictly speaking the public property of the Roman state,

---

[1] Cf the elder Seneca *controv* II I § 26, Quintilian *declam* XIII §§ 4,
11. I have given further references in my *Agricola* p 248.

[2] Lachmann, *Feldmesser* p 56.

could not be held or transferred so as to vest in the holders the highest degree of ownership[1] known to the Roman civil law. This premised, we may classify it under the following heads.

(1) Land still held and administered in the name of the Roman treasury, farmed by lessees. Its area had been large under the Republic, and was probably much less under the Empire.

(2) Land belonging to Imperial estates (what we may call Crown-lands), administered by a central bureau in Rome, which was an integral part of imperial machinery. Long before the end of the first century, the area of these estates had become enormous owing to confiscations and forfeitures of private holdings. These domains were kept quite separate from the municipal system, and free from the jurisdiction of the regular magistrates. As a rule, if not always, they were leased to tenants-in-chief, men of substance, who sublet most of the arable land to small sub-tenants, the actual cultivators. To guard against oppression, the relations of head-tenant and sub-tenants were governed by a sort of charter (*lex*) formally drawn up for each domain (*saltus*); and the enforcement of its provisions was entrusted to agents or commissioners appointed by the Emperor. These *procuratores* were generally his freedmen. An appeal against their decisions could be addressed to the Emperor. In quiet times this direct procedure was probably a great boon, for it was the ruler's interest to promote the steady prosperity of his domains, and redress of grievances might be speedy.

(3) Large estates owned by non-residents domiciled in

[1] *ager privatus ex iure Quiritium.* Cf Buckland, *Elementary Principles of Roman Private Law* §§ 34, 37.

Italy or in some Province other than[1] that in which the estate in question lay. Landholding for profit often took this form. The cases of Atticus and Agrippa carry it over from the Republic to the Empire, that of Symmachus registers its long continuance. Such estates could either be worked for owner's account by a steward directing a slave staff, or (and probably more often) through lessees free to sublet portions, perhaps under limiting conditions set out in the contract of lease. This latter plan seems to have furnished a model for the lease-conditions of imperial domains.

(4) Small holdings worked by their owners with or without slave labour (owned) or with hired labour, slave or free. These small farms were numerous in some parts of the empire. The small holdings cultivated in Egypt under an elaborate system of various tenures hardly concern me here, for it was not in Egypt that the phenomena with which I am dealing occurred.

(5) Lands included in the *territoria* of municipalities. The total area of these must have been very large. First, there were those belonging to each several community as such (*ager rei publicae*). These the town might cultivate for its own account, but the usual practice seems to have been to let them to speculators, and carry the rents to the common chest. That the larger lessees sublet portions to small men, and made a profit on the transaction, seems certain. Secondly, there were private estates, let to tenants or worked for the landlord's account. Various as the powers

---

[1] The motive of the restriction on power of buying land in a Province where a man was residing in a military or civil capacity is not quite clear to me from Dig XVIII 1 § 62 pr, XLIX 16 §§ 9, 13 (jurists of third century, first half).

of local authorities were (all ultimately derived from the constitutional charter granted to each local unit by the Roman People, that is, the central government in function), the civil jurisdiction in each territory was normally vested in its own magistrates. True, there was a general limitation forbidding them to transgress *publica lex*, the law of Rome; and some cases of importance were reserved to Roman jurisdiction, that is to the court of the Provincial governor. But in everyday affairs the local courts had a free hand.

All these Provincial lands, in principle regarded as *ager publicus populi Romani*, were subject to a land-tax, which was an important item in the Roman exchequer. Only a special grant of exemption could release them from this liability and place them on an equality with Italian land. Such grants were occasionally made, conferring on a few communities what came to be styled *ius Italicum*. These cases do not appear to have been so numerous as to make much difference to the general condition. And under the necessities of the later Empire there was a tendency to do away with all forms of exemption.

Now the contention of Heisterbergk is that agriculture was in practice promoted by direct land-taxation. It was a stimulus to effective cultivation, in order that the land so burdened might produce the amount of the tax and the largest possible surplus for the benefit of the cultivators. In Italy (and I presume in the municipalities *iuris Italici*) this stimulus was less operative. In modern England it has often been averred by men of rural experience that low rents tempt tenants to farm carelessly. There is therefore probably a certain measure of truth in Heisterbergk's contention. But it seems to me a legitimate consideration of much greater weight if we apply it to the municipal lands at the disposal of the local authorities. If and when they granted to one of themselves a beneficial lease of some *praedium rei publicae*, the mischief done might easily extend far beyond the reservation of an insufficient rent to the town chest. It might mean that the lessee, content to make a comfortable profit with little trouble to himself, would be at no pains to exert a continuous and watchful control, such as the conditions of successful agriculture demand. Sub-tenants (as experience, Irish and other, shews) are not forward to exhibit a prosperity that may invite a rise in their rents; and under such conditions the soil is not made productive up to its full capacity. If this sort of slack farming prevailed on the municipal estates, is it likely that private landlords within the municipal territory would find it easy to get their own estates turned to the best possible account? I think not. On the whole I am inclined to believe that the management of municipal[1] estates was leading even in the first century to grave abuses, and that the legislation forbidding local senators to hold leases under their own authority records an attempt to cope with an evil that might (and did) have consequences of unforeseen magnitude.

IV

I have depicted municipal magnates as inclined to use their powers over the land of their several communities for their own individual profit or convenience. I have

---

[1] O Seeck, *Untergang* II p 154 well remarks that divided responsibility (among *curiales* or *decem primi*) tended to neglect, as no one individual felt himself responsible. On p 160 he imputes much of the financial mismanagement to the subordinate clerks who were often slaves of the municipality.

just suggested that jobbery of this kind might have its
drawbacks; that the practical working of the system might
not promote the object of wringing the highest possible
returns out of land-enterprise. If, as I suggest, there was
corruption attended by disappointing results, must we not
ask why the central government did not step in more
vigorously, and make an end of a self-condemned system?
Why was it content to forbid *decuriones* to hold leases of
municipal land? When this rule was evaded, why does a
great jurist find a means of checking evasion only in the
corrective jurisdiction of *curatores* and Provincial[1] governors, open as they often were to local influence or bribes?
I think a fair answer is only to be reached by comparing
the relations of municipalities to the central power with
those of imperial domains. In both cases the imperial
interest was first of all a financial one, the collection of
dues with the least possible waste of time or energy.
Accordingly we find both the tenants-in-chief of the
Domains and the decurions of municipalities employed
in such collection, to the relief of the respective bureaus
in Rome to whom the collected amounts were paid.

But at this point an important difference meets us. If
there were at any time grounds for believing that the
management of a Domain by the chief tenant in any
respect tended to impair its productivity in years to come,
he would surely have a short shrift. No Emperor or
responsible official would knowingly condone any such
nonsense. Concealment might sometimes be bought by

---

[1] See Dig XXII 1 § 33 (Ulpian) where the duty of *praeses provinciae*
is defined as that of securing the income from taxation with the
minimum of interference. A very notable passage. Cf the rescript
cited in Dig L 1 § 38[1].

bribing a Procurator. But if the sub-tenants combined in earnest against an oppressor, the interest of the Emperor coincided with their own, and an appeal to Rome was likely to get a favourable hearing. The case of a municipality was complicated by what appears to me an inevitable consideration. If the central power dismissed the local senate, either a new set of senators must be installed in their place, perhaps no better than their predecessors: or the central power must take over the entire management of the municipal affairs, and not remain content with merely appointing a *curator*. For the latter course a new imperial staff of officials would be required. Where was a supply of fit persons to be found? And who could continuously watch them, if and when found, so as to secure their efficiency and honesty? The imperial government already had enough to do in watching its subordinate agents. It was simpler, and would save a vast amount of trouble, to let the existing authorities remain[1] in function, and to hold them liable for the punctual payment in full of the imperial dues. This seems to me a self-suggested line of argument, and its conclusion natural in the circumstances. It offers an explanation of the fact that municipal duties (*munera*), including the acceptance of office (*honores*) by men of sufficient means, are referred to[2] as being compulsory in extracts cited from Ulpian. Thus this state of things must have arisen before 228, and was apparently

[1] This seems to account for the anxiety to make owners retain their estates and so be qualified for the local *curia*. Dig L 5 § 1[2] (Ulpian) seems to shew this. For the later law see Cod Theod XII 3 § 1 (386 AD), § 2 (423 AD). In XII 11 § 1 (314 AD) we find the aim, to keep a man's estate under the lien of the *civitas* as an *obnoxium corpus*, plainly stated.

[2] Dig L 1 § 38[6] (Papirius Justus), 4 § 4[1] (Ulpian), 5 § 1[2] (Ulpian).

then established and in full operation. When we find the personal liability of local senators for the full discharge of imperial dues on behalf of their several municipalities an admitted fact, but the date of its origin undetermined, it may perhaps not be too bold to suggest that it probably arose as a sequel of Trajan's appointment of *curatores*; that is, as an attempt to give practical effect to that measure. For to get in a steady revenue from the taxes was after all the first and indispensable object. On this supposition the compulsory liability, ruinous to the municipal senates[1] under the later Empire, would have become law under one of Trajan's successors, in the glorious 'Antonine' age.

When we are told that it was a traditional Roman policy to hold the communal senates responsible for delivery of the land-tax, we can accept the statement. The laws of the Theodosian Code[2] reveal a condition of constraint and distress that can hardly have been the result of sudden change of circumstances. References in the jurists shew that compulsory tenure of onerous offices was already operative about the end of the second century, and about 112 AD Trajan gives us the first mention[3] of those *qui inviti fiunt decuriones*. But neither from previous inquirers nor from my own search can I discover any direct evidence of any legislative act[4] imposing on local senators the liability for taxes that they were unable to collect. If

---

[1] Cf Dig L 4 § 18[26, 27] (Fourth Century jurist).

[2] See for instance Cod Theod XII 1 § 186 (429 AD).

[3] Pliny *epist* X 113.

[4] In Cod Just XI 59 § 1 Constantine refers to an order of Aurelian laying on them the burden of occupying derelict lands and paying the dues thereon. But this seems a result of dire distress at the time, and in making the *civitatum ordines* liable it looks rather as if he were following an already existing custom.

we are to admit the fact of a traditional policy, I think we must not limit it to matters of finance, though it might often take effect in that connexion. To hold the leaders of a community responsible for the acts of their state is a policy writ large in the history of mankind, and needs no illustration. Rome only did as others before and since when she took bloody vengeance on the senators of Capua in the second Punic war. The internment of the Greek leaders in 146 BC was a preventive measure dictated by similar motives. An irregular instance of cruelty inspired by private greed is the affair of Scaptius, related[1] by Cicero. That agent of M Brutus, entrusted by a corrupt Provincial governor with military force, proceeded to exact an usurious and illegal debt from the city of Salamis in Cyprus. His method was to keep the local senators in confinement until payment was made, and some of them died under this treatment. Appian[2] makes M Antonius in 41 BC say to Asiatic Greeks that among the boons conferred on them by Julius Caesar was the relief from the extortions of Roman tax-farmers, by allowing them (the local communities) to collect the tribute from the cultivators of the soil. No doubt this was a great relief. But presumably some person or persons had to be responsible for delivery of the amount due. And who could these be, but the governing bodies[3] of the several cities? Then, as the municipal system developed in the early Empire, and the Republican system of tax-farming was dropped, the

[1] Cic ad Atticum v 21, vi 1, 2.   [2] Appian civ v § 4.

[3] In particular, the active committee of each local senate, the *decem primi*. In Dig L 4 § 1¹ we find *decem primatus* reckoned as a *munus patrimonii* for this very purpose (Hermogenian, mid fourth century). Cf L 4 § 18²⁶ (Charisius, same period).

tax-collecting powers of the local governments became normal, and the millstone of financial responsibility was indissolubly attached to their unhappy members. In default of evidence that this was brought about by some enactment at a certain date, I conclude that it was the result of a gradual process; probably piecemeal, as the practice became established in one municipality after another.

Thus, when we are told[1] on the authority of Papinian that the duty of collecting the *tributum* is not reckoned among the *sordida munera*, and therefore is entrusted to decurions, we seem to be placed at a moment when this point appeared sufficiently ripe and real to call for an eminent jurist's opinion. A little later, and the beginnings of flight from office in order to escape its burdens, and the compulsory pressure to counteract this movement, are attested by citations from Ulpian. What we get from these witnesses is quite consistent with the supposition of a gradual and piecemeal change. The attention of the jurists is drawn to questions arising here and there in the past working of the imperial machine; their opinions help to determine the mode of its future working. In general their influence supports the central power against local authorities. True, they shew a marked consideration for the wellbeing of the municipalities, and are careful[2] not to attribute to the imperial *curatores* excessive powers. But we cannot tell how far the well-meant definitions of the lawyers found regular expression in the practice of the officials. At all events the central power grew till it was openly an autocratic monarchy: this stage reached, it was

---

[1] Dig L 1 § 17[7]. Papinian was murdered in 212 AD.

[2] Dig XXXIX 4 § 11[1] (Paulus), L 8 § 11 (Papirius Justus).

able to take over the function hitherto performed by expert interpreters; in short to interpret its own will in a mass of laws recording its own vacillation; above all, its own failures. But as to the ruin of the helpless municipalities, and of its connexion with the ruin of agriculture, we are at least left in no doubt by the laws of the Theodosian Code.

That the intervention of an Emperor to correct abuses in municipal government was regarded as a boon[1] under the earlier Empire, is evident from the practice of transferring a Province from the charge of the Roman Senate to that of the Emperor. It was a remedy for evils due to the lax control of the Senate over its governors. In effect it placed the *Princeps*, for the purposes of a particular Province, in a position resembling that in which he stood relatively to his own Provinces—and to the Imperial Domains. Whatever the reform of municipal machinery could do to promote sound administration, that he could now do legally and promptly. I do not suggest that he could have cured all evils, let his good will have been ever so great. I do suggest that circumstances were not favourable to bold and thorough measures, and that these circumstances, mainly if not wholly, were nothing but the complications arising out of the double capacity of municipalities as (*a*) self-governing units (*b*) tax-collectors. And it is well to remember that in the Provinces there were a few 'Free' or 'Allied' states whose special exemptions left most of the taxation to rest on those not so privileged. In dealing with these the Emperor had a more free hand than the Roman Senate, and in course of time a levelling

[1] See Dr Hardy, Introduction to *Pliny's correspondence with Trajan* pp 29—49.

policy was inevitable. To the majority of municipal communities this movement would be welcome. The scruples of Trajan[1] could not and did not prevent the drift towards uniform subjection.

V

To sum up my conclusions, let me state them in the form of simple propositions as follows

The decay of the municipalities, and their conversion into mere taxation units charged with imperial burdens, is not to be fairly accounted for as the effect of centralization[2] and the growth of Roman bureaucracy since the end of the second century. For the notion that the city was the state, and that its citizens, wherever resident, could only exercise their full political rights at their civic centre, was a creed unchallenged. It dominated the Roman system from time immemorial. The decline and fall of the Republic was therefore a scene of vain struggles and helpless drifting: men could find no way to combine active citizenship with the maintenance of peaceful order. Centralization remained. But the central power, that had once been wielded by kings or by quasi-regal magistrates of the Roman People, and that in course of time had been transferred by circumstances to the Senate, needed reconstruction. Civil wars left it incarnate in the master of legions, and the history of the Principate is the tale of a long struggle ending in the inevitable conclusion, auto-

[1] Pliny *epist* x 92—3, 110—1.
[2] That the supreme power could only be in function at a given centre (Rome) is true from the earliest times. It was part of the city-state idea. The growth of *interference* is the real point, and the question is, When?

cracy. During this struggle bureaucracy was steadily developing: without it autocracy would have been impossible.

The relation of the municipal units to the central power can only be understood if we bear in mind the constitutional problem presented to Roman statesmanship, and the blindness to the lesson of the Roman past that vitiated the attempted solution. That subject units should support the imperial state, financially and otherwise, and that they should give the least possible trouble to the central government, was a situation to be desired. Three means were employed to promote these ends. First, taxation of the Provinces was moderate, if we regard it as coupled with an implied guarantee of security and order. Secondly, the military service was not an undue burden, and it offered an opportunity of gaining the privileges of Roman citizenship. Thirdly, the municipal units were left large powers of self-government in their internal affairs. Consistently with time-honoured Roman policy, these units were not all placed on the same level of privilege. So long as the public peace was not broken, intermunicipal rivalry (sometimes rising to intense jealousy) was accepted as a not unwelcome check on possible disloyalty to Rome. But the republican model of their constitutions—magistracy, senate, popular assembly—was liable to the same course of development as had formerly modified the working of the Roman constitution. The tendency was for the senate to become in practice[1] the local government. Now at Rome this tendency was offset by the responsibilities of an imperial policy, which popular assemblies could not conduct. Hence the long domina-

[1] See Reid p 448 on the eventual transfer of the powers of the Assemblies to the local senates.

tion of the Senate, only ended by the sword. But municipal senates had no share in imperial policy. Nor could they be allowed to engage in warfare on their own account. Interest in the administration of local affairs, and the ambitions connected therewith, were their preoccupations under the shelter of the Roman Peace.

That the example of the imperial city was not without influence[1] on the subordinate units is unquestionable, and this was especially true in the western Provinces, where Roman (or rather Graeco-Roman[2]) civilization made its most penetrative conquests. But the political mechanism of the municipalities seems to have worked very much as that of the Roman Republic had done on a larger scale of old. In their prosperity the cities exhibited phenomena that irresistibly remind us of Rome. A local aristocracy of office, enjoying social precedence and political power based on popular support, was concerned to secure its privileged position by munificence. In largesses, shows, outlay on public works, performance of public functions at their private expense, in charitable foundations, the upper class found means of keeping municipal government safely in their own hands. Large outgoings called for large incomes. As the nobles of early Rome had enriched themselves by monopolizing state lands, as later they and equestrian capitalists had shared the plunder of an empire, so the local magnates of the cities took advantage of their opportunities. As the benefactions of the

[1] Luxury and extravagance in these local centres and the evil effects on soldiers quartered there are to Tacitus matters of course. See *hist* I 67, II 62, III 2.

[2] The practice of professions and crafts was largely in the hands of Oriental Greeks.

Roman politicians and wealthy individuals were designed
to gratify the city populace of Rome, so too it was the
town-dwellers of the *municipia* that profited by the liberality
of local benefactors. The Roman scene has as background
the decay of Italian agriculture and the ill-starred projects
of agrarian reform. There is enough evidence bearing on
the municipal land-question to suggest that this department was suffering from abuses in the Provinces also.

But then—if there was corruption and mismanagement,
and the rustic population of municipal *territoria* suffered
from the selfish policy of urban rulers, why did not the
town population make some effort to reform a system that
only enriched the Few at the expense of the Many? That
the jobbery really tended to promote a high standard of
agriculture, I see no reason to believe: it could hardly tend
to make the rustics contented: it was much more likely
to breed irritation. But the townsmen were apathetic,
not only as enjoying the comforts and pleasures provided by the interested munificence of the rich. They were
themselves too partners in the exploitation of the countryfolk; for in some *civitates* the occupiers of land (*possessores*)
were bound to deliver[1] a fixed proportion of their produce
for sale in the town below market-price, and this burden
is even referred to as general. Thus there was no chance
of reform in land policy originating within the town. If
anything of the kind was to be undertaken, it could only
come from the central imperial power, the only power
able, and in its own interest willing, to act uncorruptly
for the general good. I have pointed out above certain
considerations that might naturally make the central power

[1] Dig VII 1 § 27[1] (Ulpian), and L 4 § 18[25] (Arcadius Charisius,
fourth century).

loth to commit itself to vigorous intervention in local administrative affairs. The measures of which we have record suggest a minimum of interference, a reluctance to undertake any responsibility that could be avoided. But they were enough to weaken the municipal governments. That they were not enough to achieve their immediate object, the sequel proved.

My main contention is therefore this, that the breakdown of the imperial system, confessed in the reconstruction of Diocletian, was due not merely to the blundering of the central government but to a combination of causes. I hold that local governments of the pattern generally adopted were from the first liable to follow a certain course of degeneration social and economic. This they did, but we get no hint of it until things had gone so far as to compel the attention of the central power. If there was an opportunity for success in remedial measures, the central power was not competent to devise them, limited as its views were by the ideas of its own time. So the result was that its treatment of a deep-seated malady was ineffective to begin with, and in the end mischievous. Nor have we good reason to believe that there was an opportunity; that there was at any stage a possibility of a happy issue out of the afflictions of the Empire, attainable by political wisdom. The inability of its passive parts to vitalize the whole, the inevitable stagnation promoted by the attempts of the centre to invigorate the parts,—these were the automatic agencies that I call the Roman Fate. That the economic problems of agriculture should have played an important part[1] in exposing the Empire's inner

[1] For the later Empire this is most clearly brought out by Seeck. But even he seems hardly to detect signs of it in the earlier period.

weakness, is surely no wonder. The long drama that opens with the claims of Plebeians to full citizenship and a share of land (the freeman's lot), ends in an universal scene of servile helplessness in which the most pitiful figure is the predial serf. If we had anything like a full record of agricultural history, I believe we should be able to trace a continuous development, a movement with temporary ups and downs, but steadily tending to a destined end. This we are not in a position to do. But it is nevertheless our duty not to be blinded by onesided evidence, and suffer urban voices to overwhelm the comparative silence of the countryside.

VI

I have stated my case from the political and economic points of view, but I am aware that there is also a moral side of it that should certainly not be ignored. To impute habitual jobbery to the ruling cliques of municipal centres is only justifiable on the assumption that the customary and legal setting of their lives was such as to facilitate and encourage a grasping and oppressive policy. Now we must, difficult though it may be, place ourselves in imagination in a world that accepted slavery as an established institution, only challenged now and then by philosophers on general humanitarian grounds. Such questioners, mostly Stoics, had little or no influence on opinion, even in Rome. Their political attitude had set the early Emperors against them. Their influence is only to be traced in the slow humanizing of the law. I can see no reason to believe that their philanthropic views had any general effect throughout the empire. The fact, that in ordinary relations of life one human being could be the chattel of another, remained and qualified the social atmosphere; and Christianity could not (or did not) repudiate it. Surely it was a hard-hearted world. True, experience had long ago discovered the economic defects of slave labour. But the discovery did not lead to its disuse. To the wealthier classes it commended itself as an appliance of comfort and luxury, even as an industrial organ capable of being turned to private profit. How the free poor viewed it, we do not know. But we do know that, supposing they did resent servile competition, they had no effective means of expressing their disapproval. That the assemblies of municipal burgesses eventually became null, and the local senates the only holders of responsibility and power, is well known. And even in the earlier period the local burgesses were kept under control by the interested benefactions of the rich, and by their own incapacity for initiating reform.

But it seems to me that the most degrading influence at work all over the Roman world was a practice[1] duly recognized and embodied in the penal law. And this can be dated from the early days of the Empire, and indeed connected with the foundation of the Principate. I refer to the practice of inflicting for the same offence different penalties on men of good social position and those of lower grade. It is not easy to conceive a characteristic feature of any civilization more damning than this. Yet such was the case with Roman citizens under the Empire. Under the Republic they were legally all on the same footing: any differences in practice were nothing more than the miscarriages that, as Mommsen remarks, no government is wholly able to avoid. But the Principate,

[1] For a convincing discussion of this subject see Mommsen, *Strafrecht* pp 1031—1037.

while depriving the Nobility of power, was constrained to create privilege. The establishment of the senatorial and equestrian Orders as privileged classes (*uterque ordo* as opposed to *plebs*) was followed by the exemption of upper-class offenders from penal servitude under Tiberius. The principle of legal differentiation thus begun was soon extended. Under Marcus, exemption from liability to torture was added, and differential treatment had evidently become a regular part of the legal system. The jurists of the Digest refer to it as a matter of course. In the Theodosian Code of the fifth century the laws of Christian Emperors fully confirm this horrid abomination, illustrating the tyrannous and cruel spirit of the age. But surely the ideas that underlay this inhuman development of penal legislation were far older than the Roman Empire, early or late. They were the logical development of a moral code that allowed the free citizen to torture his own slave, and recognized the official torture of slaves to extract evidence in courts of law. In the servile world of the later Empire it became the practice to torture the unprivileged citizen; and even the privileged, such as municipal senators, lost some of their immunity from the most degrading punishments for crime.

If anyone believes that in such a social and moral atmosphere local government by men of property could remain for generations just and beneficent, I cannot at present agree with him.

VII

If I am not grossly in error, historians of the Roman Empire are exposed to a subtle temptation that leads them unintentionally to present their story in a false perspective.

It is necessary to dwell on the Romanizing of the subject countries. The material remains, and the wealth of epigraphic record, furnish imposing details for a striking picture, true so far as it goes, and leaving an impression that it is complete. The differences of East and West are fully recognized. But I wish the difference between town and country received a more adequate recognition. Believing as I do that the rural population in the empire as a whole far outnumbered the urban, and faced with the legislative efforts of the later Emperors to keep labour on the land, producing food, I cannot believe that the condition and experiences of the rustics were of little moment in determining the destiny of Rome. However helpless and inarticulate the majority may be, a government that neglects or misrules them will sooner or later pay a heavy penalty. All the more, if they are the rustic backbone of the state. Let me assume for the present that 'Romanizing' was in effect an unifying empire-strengthening process, and confine my inquiry to the West; I ask, in what form and degree are we to view it as effective in rural districts, fostering a common Roman patriotism, solidifying the empire's man-power? I can only answer that I do not know. That imperial defence in the fourth and fifth centuries was more and more entrusted to alien soldiers, and that in the last stage the barbarian invaders took possession of Gaul and Spain with comparative ease, are surely proof enough that something was lacking; and I hold that the missing element was the cohesive force of national spirit.

Modern Biologists are beginning to assert the importance of accepting the conclusions reached by the study of heredity and of having an eye to them in all questions of national wellbeing. The pressure of this movement seems

likely to become more and more insistent. To a student
of Roman history it may suggest the question, how far
was what we call Romanizing an effective substitute for
genuine racial assimilation. Surely no serious historian
will maintain that the Provinces (meaning in particular
the West) were Romanized through racial change, by an
overwhelming infusion of Italian blood. That the Provincial populations as a whole were natives, not immigrants, is not denied. Even in Africa, where 'Roman'
settlers were numerous, the immigrants[1] were but a small
minority, as Professor Reid has pointed out. And the
veterans planted on land-allotments were not necessarily
Italians: as time went on they were more and more of
mixed or alien origin. That the Roman citizens resident
in the Provinces (*consistentes*) were mainly speculators in
financial or land-exploiting enterprises, and most of them
domiciled in the towns, is about as certain as it can be.
Near the frontiers a considerable 'Roman' influence of a
kind emanated from the great military stations and the
camp-towns (*canabae*)[2] that grew up adjoining them. But
this influence was peculiar, and tended rather to dilute the
Roman element than to strengthen it. In Britannia the
country houses (*villae*) of Roman landlords were chiefly
planted in the peaceful districts sheltered by the military
posts; and I do not believe that this was exceptional.
Now, even supposing that these landlords resided on their
estates the whole year through (which may well be doubted),
they were too isolated to Romanize native dependents in
any marked degree.

I hold that the situation, fairly viewed, suggests that the

---

[1] Reid, *Municipalities* pp 254, 257, 262, 279, 316, 322.

[2] For the beginnings of these see Tacitus *hist* IV 22.

'Roman' influence, so far as it tended to create a self-conscious imperial patriotism, superseding the perished or enfeebled self-consciousness of racial groups, was concentrated in the urban centres, and did not effectually penetrate the countryside. It was the influence of a Graeco-Roman civilization, urban to the core. The great capital set the fashions, and the Provincial cities aped them according to their several capacities. Social and literary circles followed[1] the Roman model. Lugudunum, Burdigala, Corduba, Carthage, all played a part in Latin literature, especially rhetoric, each in their time and measure; and in Rome itself literary production was largely in the hands of Provincials. The works of great writers were studied far and wide. Nothing is a more convincing proof of this than the epitaphs in verse that have come down to us. Echoes of Latin poets[2] abound in these curious compositions, and certain popular passages recur as *clichés* again and again. Vergil is of course the author favoured[3] beyond all others. But the demands of the urban and military centres are enough to account for the phenomenon. There is no reason to connect it with the native

[1] E E Sikes, *Roman Poetry* p 16 'In literature as in politics, the nerve-centres of the Empire were gathered in Rome.' This attraction was as old as the days of Ennius.

[2] See the index to Bücheler's *carmina epigraphica*.

[3] In his new (1924) History vol I pp 507—9 H Dessau gives a fine sketch of Vergil's influence in Romanizing the West. In pp 543—4 he assigns a similar influence to Livy. But he does not shew that the rustics were affected, nor do I believe it. In Claudian *de cons Stilichonis* III 138—60 and Prudentius *contra Symmachum* II 602—22 I see notable specimens of the hollow fancies acceptable to strongly contrasted literary circles about 400 AD—utterances with no true message for the actual Roman world.

rustic majority. It is surely unjustifiable to detect in literary penetration a really Romanizing influence operating on the whole population. The subject races learnt enough Latin to produce the various Romance dialects. Their racial self-consciousness was not so dead that they could not outlast a new conquest and produce 'Latin' nations.

VIII

I have been charged by a critic of my former essay with a 'complete misunderstanding of the Roman Empire.' This unhappy result he attributes to my insufficient attention to the achievements of recent epigraphic studies, from which we have gained 'a knowledge of what Romanization meant and of the feelings entertained by the provincial populations towards the Empire under which they lived.' He then refers to the flourishing condition of local life, generally municipal, in the first century, and describes it as 'gradually declining indeed but still far from extinct, until at earliest the reforms of Diocletian.' I hope I have said above enough to shew that, if I have erred, it is not from slovenly inquiry or the haste of an itching pen. I plead that there is a method, if not a reason, in my delinquency. When we both speak of 'the provincial populations,' we do not both mean the same thing. He passes over the native rustic element, which to me is the great silent force of the first importance to the Empire. Not a few Emperors seem to me to have been aware of its value, and to have tried to remedy abuses that depressed the condition of the actual cultivators of the soil. But the trend of circumstances hampered or nullified such efforts: either the measures were ill adapted to their purpose, or corruption thwarted their application, or (most fatal defect of all) they were undertaken too late. To me there seems reasonable ground for believing that among the hindrant circumstances should be reckoned the working of the municipal system: that is, that the *res publicae* were centres in which some abuses readily arose, while their relations to the central government stood in the way of timely and thorough reform.

APPENDIX

IX

I venture to add here some gleanings from the epigraphic field. They do not amount to much. In course of time the *vilici*, who had been stewards in charge of farms, seem to have become headmen of the labour staff, the general management of estates being entrusted to *actores*. These would probably be freedmen, more competent to transact business than *vilici* who were usually slaves.

Of the *coloni* and *colonae* I have to remark that the record so far as I can discover is practically confined to Italy, and that the persons are mostly, if not all, freedmen and freedwomen. It seems that the *colona* is the tenant's wife. Her recognition as joint head of the establishment is notable, and I take it to imply a position specially appropriate to the conditions of farm life. The house-mother or goodwife was a traditional figure of the good old days (the *severa mater* of Horace), and no doubt still to be found much later in the Italian highlands. Even on slave-worked estates the slave *vilicus* had a consort, the *vilica* with duties of her own. The inscriptions in most cases are purely personal, family records, and the only point of agricultural interest is that in two or three cases stress is laid on the long duration of the tenancy. It may be that this was thought exceptional and therefore worthy of record: but I hesitate to infer this from so little evidence.

Of the *coloni* of the Imperial domains I have spoken elsewhere, and have only to comment on their employment in building work. Was this service reckoned as a part of their normal labour-dues (*operae*), or was it an extra burden imposed to meet a temporary need? More likely the latter, I fancy. If so, was it a *corvée*, or were they paid for their labour? I have found no evidence to decide this point. Tacitus in a rhetorical passage makes a British chief refer to forced labour as one of the burdens laid on subjects by Rome (*Agr* 31), mentioning road-making and mining in particular. But such utterances hardly cover the case of men regularly settled as sub-tenants on a domain. The Rapidum inscription is on a different footing. The veterans planted in the Provinces were a masterful class, of great social importance under the later Empire. For a specimen of their temper see Tacitus *ann* XIV 32. That they probably contributed little to Romanize the local populations, is perhaps not too rash an inference from Tac *ann* XIV 27, though the country there referred to is Italy.

The cases cited under 'special lights' are dealt with severally. The second of them is especially interesting if, as I believe, it attests the presence of itinerant farm-labour in Africa, apparently free and wage-earning. That there were many prosperous farmers in that Province is certain, and the references elsewhere to a considerable 'plebeian' population on the land (see my *Agricola* p 341) may imply the existence of hired labour in some quantity. Certainly further evidence is to be desired.

A. *vilici* and *vilicae*.

The inscriptions in memory of *vilici* are numerous. Most are evidently slaves, some freedmen.

(1) CIL IX 3028 (district of Marrucini) Hippocrati Plauti vilic[o] familia rust[ica] quibus imperavit modeste.

(2) CIL X 5081 (Atina) C Obinius C L Epicadus Trebia ƆL Aprodisia hic vilicarunt annos XIIII. (ƆL = *mulieris liberta*.)

(3) CIL II 1552 (prov Baetica) Sabdaeus vilicus annor[um] LIII.

(4) CIL II 1742 (Gades) Gelasinus vilicus.

(5) CIL II 1980 (Baetica, Antonine age) C C N Suavis L et Faustus vilic[us] Lar[es] et Genium cum aedicula prim[i] in familia DSDD. (prim*i* or prim*um*? Mommsen points out that C C N indicates the name of the *dominus*.)

B. *actores*.

(1) Dessau 7451 (Velitrae) Tablet erected by wife actori et agricolae optimo.

(2) Dessau 7452 (Gallia Lugudunensis) erected by wife and son to Valentinus who was actor fundi Ammatiaci b[onorum] Flavi Stratonis. Compare 3761 (near Tridentum) actor praediorum Tublinatium.

C. *coloni* and *colonae*.

(1) Dessau 7453 (near Rome) Tablet erected by colonus fundo Mariano to his daughter.

(2) Dessau 7454 (Rome) erected by colonus agri Caeli aenei to his wife Anulenae Certae colonae agri s[upra] s[cripti].

(3) Dessau 7455 (district of Marsi) erected by T Alfenus Secundus patronus to T Alfenus Atticus, who is described as sevir Augustalis and colonus f[undi] Tironiani quem coluit ann[is] ñ L. (Also in Wilmanns 2501. Atticus was a freedman. ñ = *numero*?.)

(4) Dessau 7455[a] erected by the said Atticus and the familia Tironianensis to the former's wife, described as colona.

(5) Dessau 7456 (Rome) domnaedius possessor colonus sequens et tu viator precor parce tumulum Narcissi. (See Wilmanns 223, and Bücheler carm epigr 1181 (Mutina).)

(6) Dessau 8555 (Luceria) erected to T Statorio Gemino col[ono] f[undi] Pacciani by his wife Numisia Aug n ser and their filius naturalis Capriolus. (The woman apparently a slave of the imperial household.)

(7) CIL IX 3675 (district of Marsi) Atiliae...colone.

(8) CIL IX 5659 (Picenum) Q Sertorius Q L Antiochus colonus pauper fuit aequo animo scibat moriundum sibi ex testamento Balbus Antiochi L Sertoria Q L Europa Nonia Asprenatis L Helena Balbi soror in agr[o] p[edes] xvi in fro[nte] p xiiii. (An interesting case of the freedman farmer and his humble belongings. I have referred to this class in my *Agricola* p 284. Compare the case from the second century BC cited by Plin *NH* xviii 41—3.)

(9) CIL x 1877 (Puteoli) Tablet to an Augustalis—coluit annis xxxxv vixit annis lxxxiiii mens[ibus] vi dieb[us] xv.

(10) CIL x 1918 (Puteoli) to husband of Pompeia Eutychia—vixit ann lxxiiii coluit ann xxiii.

(11) CIL x 7957 (Sardinia) colonus, simply.

D. *coloni* of Imperial Domains.

To the cases dealt with in my *Agricola* pp 342—361 I add these few examples

(1) Dessau 6887 (Mauretania) Alexander Severus has erected the walls of castellum Dianese per colonos eiusdem Kastelli. (234 AD. This seems to be connected with a saltus, but it is not quite certain.)

(2) Dessau 6888 (Mauretania) under Gordian—murus constitutus a solo a colonis eius castelli Cellensis. (243 AD.)

(3) Dessau 6889 (Mauretania) Alexander again—muros paganicenses Serteitanis per popul[ares] suos fecit...etc. (populares = colonos.)

(4) Dessau 6890 (Mauretania) Altar pro salute of Severus dedicated by coloni caput saltus Horreorum et Kalefacelenses Pardalarienses. (213 AD.)

(5) CIL viii 8425 (same place in Mauretania) similar titulus to Pertinax.

(6) Dessau 6885 (Rapidum in Mauretania) under Marcus and Verus a wall built by veterani et pagani intra eundem murum inhabitantes. (This can refer to a castellum, hardly to a saltus: at least I know no reason for expecting veterans on a domain of the usual

type. The place would rather seem to be a settlement of veterans to whom land has been allotted on discharge. The pagani might be native farmers already on the spot, compelled to receive military colonists among them. But I suspect that they were not on any sort of equality with the veterans—possibly tenants under them, tillers of the old soldiers' lands. In any case I guess that the labour on the wall was mostly theirs. For paganus opposed to miles see *Agricola* p 313. For the relation that was beginning to grow up between divers classes on the ground of common residence, compare the frequent references thereto in cases of incolae. A good specimen is the inscription from Sicca in Numidia, Dessau 6818, Wilmanns 2847.)

E. Special lights on rustic circumstances.

(1) CIL IX 2438 (Samnium) An inscription giving an order addressed by Bassaeus Rufus and Macrinius Vindex (praefecti prae-torio under Marcus and Verus) to the magistrates of Saepinum, to stop the maltreatment of conductores gregum ovariaricorum, whose iumenta and pastores (expressly described as conductos) are molested, on pretext of doubtful ownership, per itinera callium, no doubt in the process of changing pastures. It is to be noted that the order lays stress on the magna fisci iniuria caused by this molestation. (Probably about 168 AD. It seems a case of survival of grazing-rights as state property, exercised by speculators under lease from the Fiscus.)

(2) CIL VIII 11824, Dessau 7457, Bücheler 1238. (Africa Byza-cena.) An epitaph in elegiac couplets, lacking the heading with formal particulars. The deceased is made to describe his own career. He was a poor farmer (ruri mea vixi colendo) from his childhood, never idle. He went out (apparently for hire) with travelling gangs of harvesters for 12 seasons, in 11 of which he was ganger. By toil and thrift he prospered, became dominus domus, owner of a villa, and lived in comfort. He became a member of the local senate (ordo) and rose from being a country bumpkin to the highest office (de rusticulo censor et ipse fui). He is thoroughly proud of his achievement. (This remarkable document is dated by expert judges not later than the third century. I note that it comes from one of the least disturbed parts of the empire. It seems inspired by the

consciousness of very exceptional success. I can cite no evidence of a case at all comparable with this.)

(3) Dessau (7742^c (Numidia) Tablet describing deceased as omnibus honoribus functus pater III equitum Romanor[um] in foro iuris peritus agricola bonus. (This I take to be an ordinary case of an urban resident who carried on a farm or farms successfully, probably under a good steward, directed and watched by his master. There is nothing surprising about it. That there were such cases in Africa other indications suggest. *Agricola* p 341.)